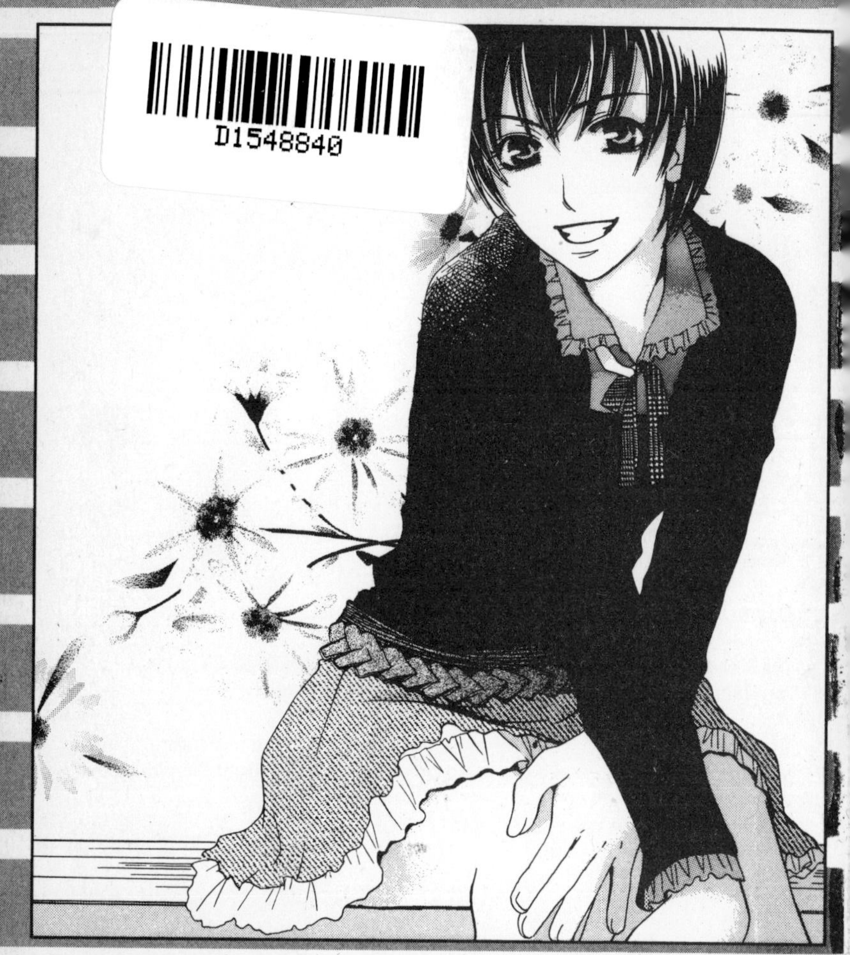

TENSHI JA NAI!!

Translation –Christine Schilling
Adaptation – Brynne Chandler
Lettering & Retouch – Jennifer Skarupa
Editorial Assistant – Mallory Reaves
Production Manager – James Dashiell
Editor – Brynne Chandler

A Go! Comi manga

Published by Go! Media Entertainment, LLC

Tenshi Ja Nai!! Volume 7

Originally published in Japan in 2006 by Akita Publishing Co., Ltd., Tokyo.
English translation rights arranged with Akita Publishing Co., Ltd.
through TOHAN CORPORATION, Tokyo.

Visit us online at www.gocomi.com
e-mail: info@gocomi.com

ISBN 978-1-933617-27-5

First printed in June 2007

1 2 3 4 5 6 7 8 9

Manufactured in the United States of America

TENSHI JA NAI!!

I'm No Angel!

Volume 7

Story and Art by

Takako Shigematsu

go!comi

Concerning Honorifics

At Go! Comi, we do our best to ensure that our translations read seamlessly in English while respecting the original Japanese language and culture. To this end, the original honorifics (the suffixes found at the end of characters' names) remain intact. in Japan, where politeness and formality are more integrated into every aspect of the language, honorifics give a better understanding of character relationships. They can be used to indicate both respect and affection. Whether a person addresses someone by first name or last name also indicates how close their relationship is.

Here are some of the honorifics you might encounter in reading this book:

-san: This is the most common and neutral of honorifics. The polite way to address someone you're not on close terms with is to use "-san." it's kind of like Mr. or Ms., except you can use "-san" with first names as easily as family names.

-chan: Used for friendly familiarity, mostly applied towards young girls. "-chan" also carries a connotation of cuteness with it, so it is frequently used with nicknames towards both boys and girls (such as "Na-chan" for "Natsu").

-kun: Like "-chan," it's an informal suffix for friends and classmates, only "-kun" is usually associated with boys. it can also be used in a professional environment by someone addressing a subordinate.

-sama: indicates a great deal of respect or admiration.

Sempai: in school, "sempai" is used to refer to an upperclassman or club leader. it can also be used in the workplace by a new employee to address a mentor or staff member with seniority.

Sensei: Teachers, doctors, writers or any master of a trade are referred to as "sensei." When addressing a manga creator, the polite thing to do is attach "-sensei" to the manga-ka's name (as in Shigematsu-sensei).

Onii: This is the more casual term for an older brother. Usually you'll see it with an honorific attached, such as "onii-chan."

Onee: The casual term for older sister, it's used like "onii" with honorifics.

[blank]: Not using an honorific when addressing someone indicates that the speaker has permission to speak intimately with the other person. This relationship is usually reserved for close friends and family.

CONTENTS

THIS STORY IS PURELY FICTION. THERE IS ABSOLUTELY NO CONNECTION TO ACTUAL PEOPLE, ORGANIZATIONS, OR EVENTS.

VOL .7

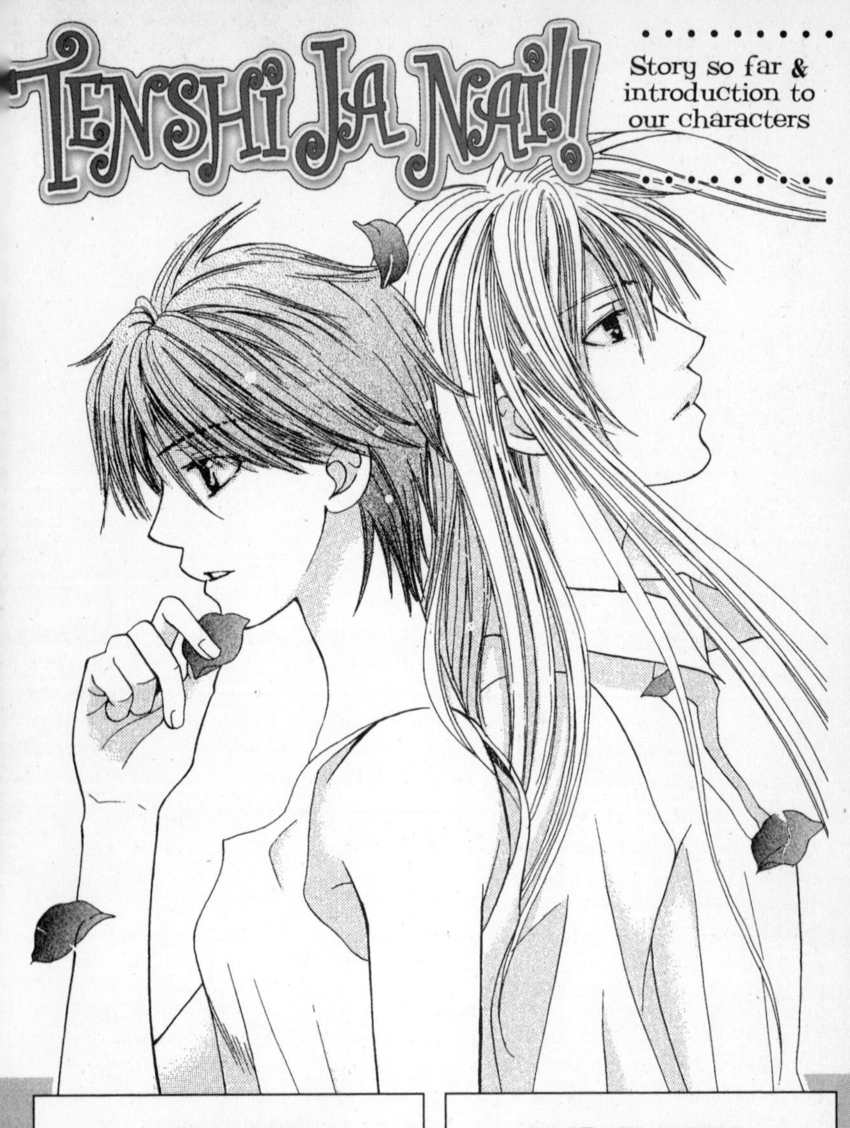

HIKARU TAKABAYASHI

She was bullied by childhood classmates who were jealous of a modeling gig she did, so she really hates being the center of attention now that she's in high school!

IZUMI KIDO

A super-popular female high schooler idol. But her true identity is a guy! In order to save his hospitalized father, he dresses like a girl and works as an idol. Very "I'm so great" type attitude.

AKIZUKI
The president of the agency Izumi is a part of. Since he's a friend of Izumi's dad, he understands Izumi's situation of having to be a girl. Quite conniving.

YASUKUNI
Izumi's public and private escort. The one who understands Izumi and Hikaru most. At the school he works as a janitor.

SAKON
Hikaru's sempai. She's in love with her cousin, Ayase, and so was Hikaru's rival. In order to recuperate from her illness, she had to leave school.

AYASE
An ex-teacher at Hikaru's school as well as her ex-boyfriend. In order to take care of his sick cousin, he left the school when his cousin did.

★Hikaru Takabayashi left her parents to live in the dorm of her all-girl's high school. She hates being the center of attention, so was horrified to find that her roommate is the super-popular high-school idol, Izumi Kido! What's worse is that Izumi's not even a girl! Once she finds out Izumi's secret, Hikaru gets pulled into helping the star at work.
★To make things even more complicated, Hikaru fell in love with the school's music teacher, Ayase. She confessed her feelings to him and they become lovers. But, when he leaves school, their relationship ends.
★Having fallen in love with Hikaru, Izumi continues to cheer Hikaru on with mixed feelings. When Hikaru starts to return Izumi's feelings, they kiss, and then...?

TENSHI JA NAI!!
I'm No Angel!

TENSHI JA NAI!!
天使じゃない!!
SCENE 31

I LOVE YOU TOO, IZUMI-SAN.
CHIRP
CHIRP
YESTER-DAY...
...WE BECAME LOVERS.
SSHHF

MORNING, IZUMI-SAN.
HOW ARE YOU FEELING?
OOH... MORNIN'.
YAWN
I'M FEELING A LOT BETTER.

THE SAME AS ALWAYS...
...THIS DIFFERENT MORNING...
UM, YOU HAVE WORK TODAY, RIGHT?
YEAH, IN THE AFTER-NOON.
DIFFERENT AS ALWAYS...
KNOCK
KNOCK
K-CLICK
EXCUSE ME.
YASU-KUNI-SAN.
SHUT
HIKARU-SAN, I NEED YOU TO MOVE OUT OF THIS ROOM.

SHFT
I OVERHEARD THE CHANGE IN YOUR RELATIONSHIP...
...OVER THE CELL PHONE, YESTERDAY. IT WAS EASY TO GUESS WHAT HAD HAPPENED.
BRISK BRISK BRISK
TO ENSURE NOTHING ELSE HAPPENS TO MAKE YOU UNABLE TO FACE YOUR PARENTS, HIKARU-SAN...
...I HAVE MADE THE NECESSARY ARRANGEMENTS.
A-ARRANGEMENTS...
LUCKILY THERE'S AN OPENING IN THE ROOM NEXT-DOOR.
HIKARU-SAN, I'M HAPPY THAT YOUR RELATIONSHIP HAS BLOSSOMED.
...I RECEIVED PERMISSION FROM THE SCHOOL TO PUT YOU THERE, SAYING THAT IZUMI'S DISORDERLY LIFESTYLE WOULD INTERFERE WITH YOUR STUDIES.
BUT...

NOW THAT WE HAVE TWO SECRETS TO PROTECT...
...WE HAVE TO BE TWICE AS CAREFUL.
SHUT
TWO SECRETS... THAT'S RIGHT...
BUT... BEING IN SEPARATE ROOMS, NOW...
SINCE IZUMI-SAN WORKS SO LATE, THIS ROOM IS THE ONLY PLACE WE CAN BE TOGETHER...
SINCE IZUMI-SAN DIDN'T ARGUE AGAINST OUR BEING SEPARATED...
HAAH ...
!
CLATTER
Sumikko's Toys
CATCH
ko's

HEY, DON'T PUSH YOURSELF SO HARD.
GASP
IZUMI-SAN!
THIS IS THE LAST OF IT, RIGHT?
THUD
Y-YEAH ...
UH... UM, LISTEN.
IZUMI-SAN, DO YOU REALLY WANT ME TO MOVE OUT?

WELL, YOU'RE ONLY GOING NEXT DOOR. WE CAN STILL SEE EACH OTHER AS MUCH AS WE WANT.

WELL YEAH, BUT ...

AND...

NOW THAT I KNOW YOU FEEL THE SAME WAY I MIGHT NOT BE ABLE TO CONTROL MYSELF.

HUH? CONTROL?

PRESS

IF YOU WANT, YOU CAN ALWAYS STAY.

SMILE

BUT YOU WON'T GET MUCH SLEEP.

I REALLY NEED MY SLEEP!!
FLEE
LOSS OF NERVE
K-CLICK
105
GASP
SLAM
IZUMI-SAN WAS TEASING ME!?
THIS ISN'T FUNNY.
I SWEAR... I CAN'T BELIEVE I'M ROOMING WITH YOU...

YOU'RE MY NEW ROOMMATE, IZUKI-SAN?
HMPH.
RRRRRIP
? ? ?
THIS IS MY SIDE OF THE ROOM SO DON'T CROSS IT, HEAR ME!?
BLOCK
AND I'M BUSY! DON'T BE TALKING TO ME ALL THE TIME!

HMPH.
I...I THINK I WANT TO GO HOME...

SIGH

I... I'M SO TIRED...

IZUKI-SAN WAS LIKE THAT ALL DAY...

IT WAS SO MUCH BETTER BEING WITH IZUMI-SAN...

KRRATTLE
YO...
GRRR
OH, WELCOME HOME, IZUMI-SAN!
YEAH, GOOD TO BE BACK... NOT!
WHY'S SUMIKKO GOTTA STAY HERE WITH ME?
WHINE
WELL, I FIGURED YOU'D BE LONELY COMING HOME TO AN EMPTY ROOM, SO...
Hmph!
I-I'M SORRY, IS SHE A BOTHER?
NO... BUT LOOK, I'M NOT LONELY...
And she snores so loud.
PHEW ...
YOU TIRED?
...A LITTLE, YEAH... BUT I'M OKAY.

FULLY CHARGED.
I-ZUMI-SAN!! WHAT IF SOMEONE SAW US!?
Heh heh.
NOBODY SAW.
G'NIGHT.

GOOD NIGHT...
I THINK I'M ALSO...
IT'S TRUE...
...FULLY CHARGED.
DIIIING
DOOOONG
CHATTER
CHATTER
IS IT JUST MY IMAGI-NATION OR ARE WE BEING STARED AT A LOT TODAY...?
I DON'T THINK IT'S YOUR IMAGI-NATION.

THE ONLY ONE BEING STARED AT IS YOU, TAKABAYASHI-SEMPAI.
AYUMU-CHAN!!
HOW ARE YOU DOING, IZUMI-CHAN?
CONGRATULATIONS ON GETTING THE ROOM TO YOURSELF.
WHY AM I THE ONLY ONE BEING STA--
FWAP
THIS!
HABAKURO'S HABASHI AGE 2
AND HIS RUMORED YOUNG GI
SOMEWHERE?
A CLANDESTINE MEETIN
IT'S TODAY'S "WEEKLY MISS."
"HABAKURO'S HABASHI (AGE 20) AND HIS RUMORED YOUNG GIRLFRIEND GOING SOMEWHERE!?"

IT WAS THAT THING FROM BEFORE...!
SHOCK
Oh, god. Oh, god.
I NEED TO TALK TO YOU, IZUMI-CHAN...
DON'T LEAVE YOUR ROOM TONIGHT.
IT MIGHT BE DANGEROUS...

I HEARD THAT THE THIRD-YEAR GIRLS ARE BRINGING IN SOME GUYS FROM THE BOYS' SCHOOL.
THE MOON CLUB'S TRYING TO STOP THEM, BUT...WE DON'T HAVE ENOUGH PEOPLE.
SINCE IZUKI-SAN'S TAKING OVER FOR THE PRESIDENT WHILE SHE'S OUT WITH A COLD, I DON'T KNOW ALL OF THE DETAILS, BUT...
...I HEARD THAT SOME OF THE BOYS ARE EXTREME FANS OF YOURS, IZUMI-CHAN.
IZUMI-SAN'S BEING TARGETED?
I SAID YOU SHOULD FORGET ABOUT IT, IZUMI-SAN!

Heh heh heh.
THEY'RE TARGETING *ME*? THAT'S RATHER COCKY OF THEM.
AND JUST WHEN I THOUGHT I MIGHT BE LOSING MY EDGE.
I'LL KILL THOSE CASANOVA WANNABES.
STRETCH
IZUMI-SAN!
I'LL DISGUISE MYSELF SO THEY WON'T FIND OUT WHO IZUMI KIDO IS.
LISTEN TO ME! DISGUISING YOURSELF AS A GUY AGAIN... SINCE IZUKI-SAN ALREADY SAW YOU IT COULD BE BAD!
... DARN.
FINE... THEN I'LL JUST GO AS IZUMI KIDO AND GET THEM THAT WAY.
IZUMI-SAN!

I'M NOT SENDING YOU AWAY.
I DON'T LIKE BEING PROTECTED BY YOU ALL THE TIME.
WORKING TOGETHER, WE CAN COME UP WITH A PLAN.
HAVING YOU ALWAYS JUST PROTECT ME...I CAN'T TAKE IT.
IZUMI-SAN...
I UNDER-STAND.

WHAT DO YOU WANT? I'M BUSY.
I HEARD ABOUT TONIGHT...
I WAS WONDERING IF IZUMI-SAN AND I COULD LEND A HAND.
YOU'VE GOT A LOT OF NERVE!
THIS IS ALL YOUR FAULT, YOU KNOW.
WHAT DO YOU MEAN?
SINCE YOU BROUGHT THAT GUY HERE...
...THE YOUNGER GIRLS WHO THINK YOU'RE "COOL" WANT TO COPY YOU.
YOU JUST LOVE MAKING TROUBLE, DON'T YOU?
I SAW YOU IN THE TABLOID-- YOU MUST BE SO PROUD!

IT'S BARELY SIX MONTHS SINCE AYASE-SENSEI DUMPED YOU, AND YOU'VE ALREADY GOT REPLACEMENTS ALL LINED UP.
LOOK, YOU DON'T HAVE TO LIKE ME...
...BUT YOU HAVE TO LET ME HELP.
THE ONLY THING THAT MATTERS ...
...IS KEEPING IZUMI-SAN SAFE.
HMPH
I GUESS I HAVE NO CHOICE.

THE TROUBLE-MAKERS' ROOMS...
...AND ALL THE DOORS IN OR OUT OF THE THIRD-YEARS' DORM HAVE HAD A NETTING INSTALLED OVER THEM.
THEY'LL BE WATCHED BY THE THIRD-YEAR SEMPAIS.
WE'VE SEARCHED OUT ALL POSSIBLE WAYS FOR THE BOYS TO GET IN.
WE'LL INCREASE THE WATCH IN THE SECOND-YEARS' DORM.
Yes, ma'am!
UM, EXCUSE ME...
YOU SAID YOU'RE SHORT-HANDED, SO CAN'T THE TEACHERS HELP?
YOU IDIOT!
IF ANY TEACHERS FOUND OUT, THEY'D TURN THIS INTO A HUGE CRISIS.

TO KEEP THE RING-LEADERS FROM BEING EXPELLED...
...THE MOON CLUB'S HANDLING IT.
HUH...
WELL, WHEN I WAS GOING TO BE EXPELLED, THEY CAME THROUGH FOR ME...
SPIN
COME ON! LET'S GO!
What're you dilly-dallying for?
EVEN THOUGH THEY DON'T LIKE ME...
BZZZT
IZUKI-SAN, WE JUST CAUGHT SOME BOYS SNEAKING INTO THE THIRD-YEARS' DORM...
PHEW
HUH, THAT WAS OVER FASTER THAN I'D THOUGHT...
AW, NO FUN.
BUT, TWO OF THEM GOT AWAY, AND WE CAN'T FIND THEM.
THEY'RE RABID IZUMI-SAMA FANS AND ARE PROBABLY HEADED THAT WAY.
Gah!

DID EVERYONE HEAR THAT? WE HAVE TWO BOYS ON THE LOOSE! TEAMS OF TWO SEARCH FOR THEM!
WAIT!
I HAVE AN IDEA.
HIKARU?
HMPH
NOW, SUMIKKO! GO FIND THE BOYS! FIND BOYS!!
LAUNCH
CHOMP
Here's one!
S-SUMIKKO!! I SAID "BOY"!
Ow ow!
Sorry, guys.
ANYWAY, YOU SHOULD STAY OUT OF SIGHT, KIDO-SAN.

DRAG DRAG
COME ON, WE'RE GOING TO THE MANAGER'S OFFICE.
HUH!? WAIT A--
I WAS JUST THINKING MAYBE WE SHOULD WATCH IZUMI-SAN'S ROOM...
SINCE THEY MIGHT TRY TO TAKE SOME OF HER STUFF...
OKAY, WE'LL GO ON PATROL.
AH...
GLARE
WHAT IS IT, NOW!?
UH... WELL...
THAT'S A GOOD POINT.
LET'S GO!
PHEW
R-RIGHT.

CLICK
CLICK
CLICK
IZUMI-SAN... I HOPE YOU CAN BE GOOD AND LAY LOW...
CLICK
CLICK
...I'M SORRY.
HUH?
FOR WHAT I SAID... ABOUT YOU AND AYASE-SENSEI.
IT'S BARELY SIX MONTHS SINCE AYASE-SENSEI DUMPED YOU...
OH, YEAH... IT'S OKAY.
I'M NOT BEING SARCASTIC. I'M REALLY WARNING YOU.
SNEAKY, SECRET RELATIONSHIPS NEVER LAST LONG.

......
SNEAKY, SECRET RELATIONSHIPS, HUH?
THIS IS IT, RIGHT?
104
K-CLICK
I'LL MAKE SURE IT'S ALL CLEAR INSIDE.
YOU KEEP WATCH OUT HERE.
SHUT
I HOPE THOSE BOYS HAVEN'T BROKEN IN...
K-CLICK
IS EVERYTHING ALL RIGHT?
YEP. ALL SAFE IN HERE.

PHEW
YEAH...? THAT'S GOOD.
YEAH... REAL GOOD...
OKAY, I'LL GO CHECK THE OTHER ROOMS.
WHISPER
SHE GONE?
WHISPER
YEAH, SHE LEFT.
YOU STAY QUIET AND WE WON'T DO ANY-THING TO YOU.
THERE WE GO. NICE AND TIGHT.
THUD
!!
STICK HER IN THE BATHROOM.

SO THIS IS IZUMI-CHAN'S ROOM, EH?
HEY! I FOUND HER PANTIES! HER PANTIES!
FWUMP
WE COULD SELL THEM...
HEY, WHAT'S THE MA--
!!
WHAM
GET YOUR FILTHY HANDS OFF IZUMI-SAN'S THINGS!
TCH! GUESS WE'LL HAVE TO KEEP YOU QUIET FOR A WHILE TOO--!
LEAP
AND ANOTHER THING...
BASH
BROOM
IZUKI-SAN ISN'T STUPID ENOUGH TO CHECK A ROOM WITH THE LIGHTS OFF!

IZUKI-SAN WOULD NEVER SMILE AT ME!
WHACK
STERN
AND JUST SO YOU KNOW, OUR GYM TRAINING INCLUDES KARATE.
MESSING WITH BOYS WILL HURT YOU MORE THAN US, YOU KNOW!
GRAB
Oof!
OH, NO!!
HEY, LET'S GET A PAIR OF PANTIES FROM THIS GIRL, TOO!
WITH A PHOTO OF HER FACE, IT'D SELL BIG IN THE BURUSERA*.
GREAT IDEA!
!!
DON'T TOUCH ME!! I'LL SCREAM!
DO YOU HAVE ANY IDEA HOW MANY GIRLS YOU'D NEED TO STOP US?

*SEE TRANSLATOR'S NOTES

NO!
IZUMI-SAAAAAAAN!!
EEEEEEK
SHUT UP! QUIET, YOU LITTLE...!
WHIP

SMACK
THUD
WHAT THE ...!?
WHO'S THERE !?
SSHET
IT DOESN'T MATTER WHO'S HERE.
GET YOUR FILTHY HANDS OFF HIKARU.

SHOVE
HEY!
STEP
CRACK
STOMP
YOU GO TO SLEEP.

HIKARU, ARE YOU OKAY?
IZUMI-SAN... YEAH, I'M OKAY.
THANKS FOR SAVING ME.
HARD TO IGNORE A CRY FOR HELP THAT LOUD.
OH... I'M SORRY. I HOPE I DIDN'T MAKE ANYONE SUSPICIOUS OF YOU...
NAH. I TOLD THEM YOU TOOK CARE OF THOSE GUYS, HIKARU.
AND...
I WAS VERY HAPPY.

THAT YOU CALLED MY NAME.
IT WAS THE FIRST NAME I THOUGHT OF...
IZUMI-SAN, I'M WORRIED...
...ABOUT OUR RELATION-SHIP...

IZUMI-SAN, YOU HAVE SO MANY SECRETS.
AND WE HAVE TO HIDE OUR TRUE FEELINGS FROM SO MANY PEOPLE.
I WONDER HOW LONG WE CAN STAY TOGETHER LIKE THIS...
BUT JUST LIKE I COULDN'T HELP CALLING YOUR NAME...
...I CAN'T HELP LIKING YOU SO MUCH, IZUMI-SAN.
I THINK MY FEELINGS WILL JUST SPILL OUT ANY SECOND...
AND THAT MIGHT PUT YOU IN JEOPARDY, IZUMI-SAN...
HIKARU...

SO...
SINCE I HAVE TO KEEP MY FEELINGS HIDDEN...
...I WANT TO KEEP THEM FROM BUILDING UP AND SPILLING OVER BY NEVER HIDING THEM FROM YOU, IZUMI-SAN.
HUG
THERE'S NO NEED TO WORRY, YOU SILLY.

HAVE I BEEN MAKING HER WORRY?
I-IZUMI-SAN, SOMEBODY WILL SEE US.
I DON'T CARE!
IZUMI KIDO'S HUGGING HIKARU FOR HAVING SAVED HER.
End of Scene 31

TENSHI JA NAI!!
TEXAS
ZSFW126
天使じゃない!!
SCENE 32

IT'S BEEN ONE WEEK SINCE SUMMER VACATION STARTED.
Yeah, yeah... HOW GREAT...
IT'S SO MUCH COOLER BY THE WATER!

GO AHEAD, HAVE FUN... FOR US BOTH.
GRUMBLE
YOU DON'T HAVE TO STOP JUST TO COME TO WORK WITH ME TOMORROW.
GRUMBLE
GRUMBLE
DON'T GET ALL HOT AND GROUCHY...
I'LL ONLY BE TWO DAYS LATE GETTING TO THE SHOOTING LOCATION.
THE MOON CLUB'S FORCING ME TO HELP THEM OUT. THERE'S NOTHING I CAN DO ABOUT IT.
SORRY.
PHEW
YOU KNOW HOW I GET WHEN I KNOW I HAVE TO WORK WITH KUROBE AGAIN...
SO YOU SAY... YOU CAN'T HATE KUROBE-SAN THAT MUCH.
BZZZZ
BZZZZ
WELL, NOT IF HE KEEPS HIS DISTANCE.

LISTEN.
HABASHI WILL BE COMING TO THE FILMING, TOO.
YOU'RE THE ONE WHO NEEDS TO MAKE SURE YOU DON'T GIVE HIM AN OPENING.
I-I DON'T GIVE HIM OPENINGS!
YOU TEND TO GET SWEPT UP IN THINGS, THAT'S ALL.
JUST BE PREPARED! PREPARED!
POKE
POKE
Ow ow ow!
TH-THAT'S NOT TRU--
HIKARU-SAAAAN!
OH, CHISATO-SAN.
I'M SORRY I'M LATE.
CHANGING TOOK LONGER THAN I EXPECTED.

OH, YOU'RE NOT GOING TO SWIM, IZUMI-SAN?

YEAH, I CAN'T RISK GETTING SUN-BURNED.

BZZZT BZZZT

....

WELL, I'LL GO GET US SOME DRINKS OR SOME-THING.

Hee hee.

IT MUST BE HARD BEING A CELEBRITY.

YEAH...

HAAH ...

CLATTER

THAT HIKARU... SHE JUST DOESN'T GET IT.

GRUMBLE

SHE JUST ISN'T WARY ENOUGH AROUND GUYS...

GRUMBLE

OH, IZUMI KIDO-SAN!

!?

LONG TIME NO SEE.
SINCE I WAS IN THE AREA, I GOT NOSTALGIC AND DROPPED BY.
AYASE...!!

IZUMI-SAN, WHAT'S TAKING SO LONG?
!
SEN-SEI...
...TAKA-BAYASHI.

YANK
!!
IZUMI-SAN...?
YOU'RE LOOKING WELL, KIDO.
YES I AM, THANK YOU.

IZUMI-SAN...?
Cafeteria
CHATTER
CHATTER
SEMPAI, ARE YOU FEELING BETTER?
Yay!
Wow!
WE LOVE THE LETTERS YOU SENT US, SEMPAI.
THANKS. I'M SO GLAD TO SEE EVERYONE AGAIN.
CHATTER
WHAT A BIG FUSS...
CHATTER

I NEVER EXPECTED TO SEE SENSEI THIS SOON.
I WONDER WHAT... IZUMI-SAN THINKS OF ALL THIS.
CLATTER
IZUMI-SAN?
SORRY... I'M NOT VERY HUNGRY.
OH... I'LL GO TOO THEN.
I CAN'T WAIT FOR THE UP-COMING SHOOT.
I HEARD IT'LL BE BY THE OCEAN.

THOUGH THEY WON'T BE USING SUMMER AS THE BACK-DROP--
HIKARU.
YOU AND I STARTED GOING OUT...
...WHEN AYASE LEFT.
WHAT'S... THE MATTER, IZUMI-SAN?
NOTHING... I WAS JUST THINKING...

IF AYASE HADN'T GONE BACK TO SAKON...
...HOW WOULD THINGS HAVE TURNED OUT...?
TH-THAT...
....
I'M SORRY... FOR SOUNDING WEIRD...
N-NOT AT ALL.
LET'S GO BACK TO THE ROOM.
SURE...

LISTEN.
ARE YOU SURE YOU CAN'T COME TO WORK WITH ME TOMORROW?
I WONDER IF IT'S BECAUSE ...
YEAH... I'LL COME.
I'LL GET SOMEONE TO COVER FOR ME TOMORROW MORNING.
I HAD NO ANSWER TO WHAT IZUMI-SAN SAID EARLIER...
EVEN THOUGH I'M HOLDING ONTO HIM SO HARD...
...I'M STILL SO WORRIED...

CHIRP
CHIRP
LET'S SEE, I'VE GOT TO TELL IZUKI-SAN AND AYUMU-CHAN I'M GOING, THEN...
She's gonna be so mad...
RATTLE
TAKABA-YASHI?
OH... SENSEI. GOOD MORNING.
MORNING... BUT I'M NOT YOUR SENSEI ANYMORE.

...ARE YOU DOING WELL?
--YES.
I KNEW IT.
GASP
MINORI?
OH... SEMPAI. GOOD MORNING.
YOU THINK I DON'T KNOW WHAT'S GOING ON?
EVEN WHEN I WAS IN THE HOSPITAL, I HEARD ALL ABOUT IT.
MINORI, STOP IT.

I KNOW ALL ABOUT YOU AND TSUKASA-NIISAMA GOING OUT IN SECRET!
IS THIS THE SAME SAKON-SEMPAI?
ARE YOU HURT?
I WILL WIN HIS LOVE, NOT AS HIS LITTLE SISTER, BUT AS A GROWN-UP WOMAN.

GULP
SEMPAI, THAT--
BEHAVE YOURSELF, MINORI!
WHAT HAPPENED BETWEEN TAKABAYASHI AND ME IS OUR BUSIN-NESS...
FROM THE PAST.
AND MORE IMPORTANTLY, SHOULDN'T YOU BE RESTING IN BED?
JERK
LET GO OF ME!
I'M NOT A CHILD.
I CAN GET TO BED BY MYSELF.
SEN-SEI...

...I'M SORRY, TAKABA-YASHI.
NO PROB-LEM...
WHAT'S HAPPENING HERE?
THAT'S NOTHING FOR YOU TO WORRY ABOUT.
MORE IMPORTANTLY, ARE YOU PACKED?
AKIZUKI'S PICKING US UP AT NOON.
Y-YEAH... BUT...

I JUST CAN'T BELIEVE IT...
NOT JUST HER REACTION TO ME, BUT...
...SAKON-SAN TAKING THAT ATTITUDE WITH SENSEI...
I WONDER IF SOMETHING HAPPENED BETWEEN THEM...
HIKARU.
IT HAS NOTHING TO DO WITH US.

WHATEVER'S GOING ON BETWEEN THOSE TWO IS FOR THEM TO FIX.
IT'S NONE OF YOUR BUSINESS.
...YEAH.
YOU'RE RIGHT.

THUD
CLUNK
LET'S SEE, I'VE GOT MY BATHING SUIT AND THREE PAIRS OF UNDER-WEAR...
Ready for take off
ZZZZZ
SUMIKKO... YOU'RE GOING WITH YASUKUNI-SAN.
I don't wannaaaa!
TMP
TMP
TMP
TMP
TAKABAYASHI-SAN! WHAT'S THIS ABOUT HANDING OFF YOUR WORK TO ME!?
BAM
SHOCK

WHAT'S WITH THIS MEMO !?

I need you to take ov

for

please

Hikaru Takabayashi

I-I'M SORRY. I'LL MAKE IT UP TO YOU WHEN I GET BACK!

THAT'S NOT THE PROBLEM!!

EEEEEEEK!

SHAKE SHAKE

LEAVING SEMPAI AND AYASE-SENSEI NOW WILL BE TROUBLE!

HUH?

HOW WOULD IZUKI-SAN KNOW SOMETHING LIKE THAT?

IT'S BACKFIRED. ALL OF IT...

WHAT I DID TRYING TO HELP BRING THEM CLOSER.

IT'S ALL MY FAULT.

To those I'm meeting for the first time and those I haven't seen in a while, hello! Thank you for picking up "Tenshi Ja Nai!!" volume 7. Already the 7th volume... The story will be reaching the end very soon...

We're getting very close to the climax.

From here on in I'll be more and more diligent, so please stick with Hikaru and Izumi to the very end!

KNOWING HOW SEMPAI FELT ABOUT SENSEI...

...WHEN SHE HAD TO LEAVE SCHOOL ...

...I COULDN'T STAND SEEING YOU AND SENSEI GETTING CLOSER...

...SO I MADE SURE THAT SEMPAI WOULD COME BACK RIGHT AWAY BY...

...SENDING HER A LETTER ABOUT YOUR CLOSE RE-LATIONSHIP WITH SENSEI...

BUT I WAS STUPID... I NEVER THOUGHT SHE'D TRY TO COME BACK WHILE SHE'S STILL SO SICK.

IZUKI-SAN...

I HAVE TO HELP FIX THEIR STRAINED RELATIONSHIP.
AND YOU HAVE TO HELP ME!
...BUT I'M GOING WITH IZUMI-SAN...
BUT I STILL HAVE A LITTLE TIME...
...I'LL HELP HOWEVER I CAN.

GET SENSEI TO TELL YOU HIS SIDE OF IT...
...AND I'LL DO THE SAME WITH SEMPAI.
GOT IT.
AND ALSO...
I OWE YOU ONE.
!
PHEW ...
SHHH HAAA
OKAY.
HERE I GO!

SENSEI.
TAKABA-YASHI?
MORN-ING.
GOOD MORNING.
?
Uuh...
HOW SHOULD I BREAK THE ICE?
U-UM... IS SAKON-SEMPAI'S HEALTH FAILING, AGAIN?
YEAH. THE SURGERY WAS A SUCCESS, BUT...
...HER POSTOPERATIVE PROGRESS HASN'T BEEN SO GOOD...

HER DOCTORS SAY SHE CAN BE MENTALLY UNSTABLE, SOMETIMES.
I DON'T THINK I'M STRONG ENOUGH FOR HER...
I JUST CAN'T GIVE HER THE SUPPORT SHE NEEDS...
NOW SHE'S SAYING SHE WANTS TO GO BACK TO THE HOSPITAL.
IF IT MEANS GETTING HER BACK THE WAY SHE WAS, I'M GLAD, BUT...
IT'S NONE OF YOUR BUSINESS.
BUT IZUMI-SAN...

...IT IS MY BUSINESS...
GRIp
IF I CAN HELP, I HAVE TO TRY...
I MAY BE TOO SENTIMENTAL, BUT I...
...WANT SENSEI TO BE HAPPY!!
BZZZT
BZZZT
WHAT'S THE MATTER? YOU SEEM IRRITATED TODAY.

I'M NOT IRRITATED.
OH, HOOO. I KNOW WHAT IT IS!
NOD
NOD
YOU HAD A FIGHT WITH HIKARU-CHAN, DIDN'T YOU!
GRIN
AW, YOUNG LOVE.
THAT'S NOT IT!
THEN WHAT? SPILL IT.
UNCLE HERE'LL GIVE YOU ADVICE.
EH?
......
YESTERDAY THIS EX-TEACHER NAMED AYASE CAME BACK.
AND, HE JUST HAPPENS TO BE THE GUY THAT HIKARU LIKED SIX MONTHS AGO.

Hm hm.
I SEE... SO THAT MAKES YOU UNEASY DOES IT, IZUMI-KUN?
LOOK, IT'S NOT LIKE HIKARU HAS FEELINGS FOR HIM ANYMORE.
Tsk tsk tsk. YOU'RE SO NAIVE.
IRK
THE THING ABOUT GIRLS IS THIS. THEY NEVER REALLY GET OVER PEOPLE THEY USED TO LIKE.
ESPECIALLY NOT A FIRST LOVE.
Not like I know this was her first love.
IZUMI-KUN, WHERE'RE YOU GOING?
TURN
I CAN'T HANG AROUND YOU FOR TOO LONG.
HIKARU'S LATE, SO I'M GOING TO GET HER.
UH-OH...
I wonder if I teased him too far.

SPLASH
SPLISH
I'VE GOTTA GO TELL HIM...
SPLASH
SO THAT IZUMI-SAN WILL UNDER-STAND.
HAAH...
HIKARU!
WHAT'RE YOU DOING OVER THERE?
WHERE'S YOUR STUFF?
IZUMI-SAN...

WHATEVER. YASUKUNI CAN BRING YOUR STUFF.
WE'VE GOTTA HURRY OR--
PULL
IZUMI-SAN, LISTEN TO ME!
I CAN'T GO WITH YOU TODAY.

BUT, I'LL STILL BE THERE IN TWO DAYS WITH YASU-KUNI-SAN LIKE WE PLANNED, SO--
IS IT...
...BECAUSE OF *THOSE TWO*?
YES...
I THINK SAKON-SEMPAI CAME BACK TO SEE ME...
I CAN'T JUST LEAVE HER NOW...
BECAUSE, IT'S NOT LIKE THE PROBLEM BETWEEN SEMPAI AND SENSEI HAS NOTHING TO DO WITH ME.
HOW *HONOR-ABLE*.

DO WHATEVER YOU WANT.
IZUMI-SAN!
End of Scene 32

TENSHI JA NAI!!

天使じゃない!!

SCENE 33

DO WHATEVER YOU WANT.
IZUMI-SAN WAS ANGRY, BUT IT SEEMED LIKE HE WAS ALSO HURTING...

AFTER ALL THAT... COULD I HAVE BEEN...
HAAH...
...SOMEHOW WRONG...?
SEEING IZUMI-SAN MAKE THAT FACE AT ME...
Haaah...
TAKABA-YASHI-SAN, PERFECT TIMING.
OH... IZUKI-SAN.
SAKON-SEMPAI'S ALONE IN THE STUDENT COUNCIL ROOM!

WELL? DID YOU ASK SAKON-SEMPAI ABOUT HER AND SENSEI?

I DIDN'T ASK.

DIDN'T YOU GO SO YOU COULD ASK HER!?

Like about Sensei or her health!

YOU...! IDIOT, I CAN'T ASK HER ***THAT***!

SAKON-SEMPAI'S MY IDEAL! I CAN'T ASK HER SOMETHING SO PER-SONAL!

WHAT IF SHE HATED ME FOR IT!?

Idiot!

Fool!

THEN WHY'D YOU EVEN GO!?

YOU ASK HER!

SHOVE

どん

WHOA!

!?

TAKABA-YASHI-SAN.

AH...

SAKON-SEMPAI...

AAAAND SO BEGINS THE WWWWACKY TRIATHLON RACE!! GO!!!
☆

I HATE GAMES WHERE YOU GET PUNISHED WHEN YOU LOSE!!
There's nothing funny about double-ended bungee stunts!
SPLASH SPLASH
KUROBE, ARE YOU NOT PULLING YOUR WEIGHT!?
You're the one who said we should do this!
Wacky Triathlon
I WONDER, WHICH ONE LADY LUCK IS SMILING DOWN ON?
AFTER THEY SWIM THEIR LAP UP AND DOWN THE POOL, THEY'LL COMPETE IN THE BICYCLE RACE. BUT FIRST, IZUMI-CHAN...
THAT'S RIGHT! BEFORE THAT...
...WE'RE GOING TO PUT PIRANHAS IN THERE WITH THEM! ♡
SPLISH
SPLASH

OOOOOKAY! AND THE PIRANHAS ARE OFF!
Yeah yeah yeah!
Wacky Triathlon
THUMP
SPLASH
SPLASH
SPLASH
CHOMP CHOMP CHOMP
ARE YOU GUYS CRAZY!?!?
You wanna kill us!?!?
NOW THEN, IZUMI-CHAN, LET'S STAY ONE STEP AHEAD AND MAKE OUR WAY TO THE NEXT RELAY POINT.
YES, LET'S GO.
OKAY, CUT.
ONCE YOU TWO ARE READY PLEASE HURRY TO THE CAR.
YES, SIR!
CHATTER
CHATTER
CHATTER
IZUMI-CHAN, THIS IS THE "AVERSION WITHOUT EVEN TRYING SHOWDOWN" TO BE HELD IN THE HOTEL AFTERWARD.
AH, OKAY. I'LL HAND IT OVER.
THUMP
PHEW...

I CAN'T GO WITH YOU TODAY.
BECAUSE, IT'S NOT LIKE THE PROBLEM BETWEEN SEMPAI AND SENSEI HAS NOTHING TO DO WITH ME.
IZUMI-CHAN, HURRY UP.
AH, YES SIR!
SIGH
LET HER DO WHATEVER SHE WANTS!

STOP PRETENDING YOU CARE...
HUH?
U-UM... SEMPAI, HOW ARE YOU FEELING, HEALTH-WISE?
I'M FED UP WITH...
...YOU AND AYASE-SENSEI FORCING YOURSELVES TO PITY ME.
TH-THAT'S NOT TRUE... SENSEI AND I NEVER INTENDED THAT--
"SENSEI AND I"?
I GUESS I WAS WRONG FOR SAYING YOU'RE HIS EX-GIRLFRIEND.
YOU CLAIM TO KNOW WHATEVER HE'S THINKING?
NO, THAT'S--

YOU SHOULDN'T HAVE COME HERE.
DO YOU HAVE ANY IDEA WHAT IT'S LIKE TO KNOW THE PERSON YOU LOVE IS ONLY WITH YOU OUT OF OBLIGA-TION?
...NO MATTER WHAT I DID...
NO MATTER WHAT SELFISH THINGS I SAID OR HOW MUCH I CRIED...
...HE WOULDN'T TELL ME ANYTHING...

IT'S LIKE HE WAS NEVER REALLY WITH ME...
SEMP--
SMACK
!!
I SWEAR... IF IT WEREN'T FOR YOU...
SE- SEMPAI!
YOU CAN HAVE AYASE-SENSEI.

SLAM
SEMPAI !?
SSHFFLE
!
I loved you.
Hikaru Takabayashi
I THOUGHT ...
...I COULD DO SOME-THING.

WHATEVER'S WRONG BETWEEN THOSE TWO IS FOR THEM TO FIX.
IT'S NONE OF YOUR BUSINESS.
IZUMI-SAN WAS RIGHT!
Janitor's Room
IS THAT SO?
I GOT IN THE MIDDLE OF IT AND MADE SEMPAI MAD.
AND IZUMI-SAN'S MAD AT ME TOO...

I JUST... THOUGHT THAT MAYBE I COULD HELP...
THAT WAS A PRETTY CONCEITED THOUGHT.
Y-YASU-KUNI-SAN?
WELL, I THINK THAT YOUR SOFT HEART IS A GOOD THING, HIKARU-SAN.
STROKE
STROKE
WHAT'S IMPORTANT IS THAT YOU KEEP YOUR PRIORITIES STRAIGHT.

PRIORITIES... EH?
YOU'RE COMING HERE TOMORROW?
YES, YASUKUNI-SAN'S BRINGING ME IN THE MORNING.
REALLY? THAT'S GREAT!

SEE, I'VE GOT SOME-THING I NEED TO ASK OF YOU, HIKARU-CHAN!
THERE IS?
WHY... DO I HAVE A BAD FEEL-ING...?
UM...IS IZUMI-SAN THERE?
OH, IZUMI-KUN?
WELL, IZUMI-KUN'S IN THE BATH RIGHT NOW AND CAN'T COME OUT.
UH, YEAH.
I... SEE... OKAY...
I REALLY WANTED TO TALK TO HIM...

CH-CLICK

SLAP ばし

OKAY! TIME TO GET READY FOR TO-MORROW!

Yeah!

STARE

SUMIKKOOO! WHERE AAAAARE YOOOOU !?

WHY IS IT THAT SHE'S NEVER HERE WHEN IT MATTERS?

ALL MY STUFF'S PACKED ALREADY...
I WON'T HAVE TIME TO LOOK FOR SUMIKKO TOMORROW, SO I NEED TO GET A HOLD OF HER NOW...
MUTTER
MUTTER
ENOUGH ALREADY! STOP PLAYING AROUND AND COME OUT!!
Heh heh...
TAKABAYASHI, THAT YOU? WHAT'RE YOU DOING UP?
W-WELL, MY DOG'S ON THE LOOSE...
DOG?
OH, SENSEI!
YEAH... UH...
SPRING
?

TOMORROW I'M JOINING IZUMI-SAN AT HER WORK.
I SEE...

PHEW... SOME-HOW...
...THAT FELT GOOD...
WELL, I'VE GOTTA FIND SUMIKKO ...
TMP TMP TMP TMP
TAKABA-YASHIIIIIII!
TMP
WE'VE GOT A CRISIS!
TMP
TMP
OH, SENSEI YOU'RE HERE! IT'S AN EMERGENCY!
POINT
HUFF HUFF
W-WHAT'S WRONG?
SAKON-SEMPAI'S GONE MISSING!
WHAT!?

ARE YOU SURE SHE DIDN'T JUST GO FOR A WALK?
SHE HASN'T TAKEN HER MEDICINE AND NOBODY'S SEEN HER SINCE DINNER-TIME.
I'M TRYING NOT TO GET INVOLVED, BUT THINGS KEEP HAPPENING...
COME HELP US LOOK, TAKABA-YASHI-SAN.
O-OKAY.
GOT YOU!!!
WHY'RE YOU FOOLING AROUND NOW!?

1076791266

S-SUMIKKO, CAN YOU FIND SAKON-SEMPAI?
SNORT
RUSTLE
SNIFF SNIFF SNIFF
SPLASH
THAT SOUNDS LIKE WATER ...?

KER SPLASH
WH-WHAT'RE YOU--
SPLISH
SEMPAI!
SPLASH
SPLASH
WHAT'RE YOU DOING?
EVEN IN SUMMER THE NIGHTS ARE COOL... YOU'LL GET A CHILL!
AND DON'T YOU NEED TO TAKE YOUR MEDICINE?
IT'S MY BODY, I'LL DO AS I LIKE!!

AS YOU LIKE...? SENSEI AND IZUKI-SAN AND EVERYBODY'S WORRIED ABOUT Y--
I DIDN'T ASK THEM TO WORRY ABOUT ME.
FLUSH
SLAP
SHOCK

YOU SPOILED BRAT!!
I'M NOT SCARED OF YOU NOW AT ALL!
WHA--?
YOU'VE SLAPPED ME IN THE FACE BEFORE, BUT...
...YOU'RE TOO WEAK TO FIGHT BACK NOW, RIGHT?
Ha!

IT'S JUST LIKE YOU SAID.
YOU DON'T *DESERVE* WORRY OR SYMPATHY FROM ANY-BODY!
YOU PITIFUL, MISERABLE, SPOILED BR--
はしっ
SLAP
YOU DON'T KNOW HOW I FEEL!
NO, I DON'T!
BUT DO YOU KNOW WHAT IT'S LIKE...
...TO BE REJECTED BY THE ONE YOU LOVE MOST?

GASP
!
I'VE ALREADY BEEN REJECTED.
……
SO I DON'T KNOW WHAT HAPPENED AFTERWARD.
WHY SENSEI'S BY YOUR SIDE, SEMPAI.
IF IT'S OUT OF SYMPATHY OR OBLI-GATION...
...OR SOMETHING MORE THAN THAT...

BECAUSE HE...
...IS ALREADY FAR OUT OF MY REACH.

RUSTLE
WAIT A...! SEMPAI!
SAKON!

SEMPAI, WHAT'RE YOU DOING IN THE WATER? TAKABA-YASHI, YOU--!
EEEEE!
YOU'RE HERE, FINALLY...

COME NOW, SEMPAI. LET'S GET YOU OUT OF THE WATER.
SPLASH
SPLASH
Hurry now.
SEMPAI'S FINE.
SHE'S WELL ENOUGH TO THROW A MEAN SLAP.

TAKABA-YASHI!! LISTEN, YOU--!
OKAY, I'M SORRY.
SAKON, ARE YOU ALL RIGHT?
... YEAH ...
GASP
T-TAKABA-YASHI-SAN!
I'M LEAVING EARLY TOMORROW SO I HAVE TO SAY GOOD-BYE HERE.
TAKE CARE, YOU TWO.
B-BUT, ARE YOU REALLY OKAY WITH THAT? YOU--

YOU HAVE TO GO QUICKLY...
...TO BE WITH THOSE PRECIOUS TO YOU.
SHAKE
SHAKE
SHAKE

WHAT'S IMPORTANT IS THAT YOU KEEP YOUR PRIORITIES STRAIGHT.
I'M SURE THAT THAT...
...MEANS NOT LOSING SIGHT OF THE PERSON MOST PRECIOUS TO YOU.
I STILL HAVEN'T...
...LOST SIGHT OF IZUMI-SAN... HAVE I?

VIPHOTEL
SQUEAL
I'LL GET THE LUGG-AGE.
YOU GO FIND IZUMI-SAMA, HIKARU-SAN.
UH, OKAY.
COME ON, SUMIKKO. LET'S GO.
WOOF
Phew...
I HAVE TO APOLOGIZE TO IZUMI-SAN!
!
BOOM
はったーん
CHATTER
CHATTER
HIKARU ...

U-UM...
I, YOU
SEE,
IZUMI-
SAN...

FLASH

Flash?
Aaaaw...
NO GOOD.
HIKARU-CHAN,
YOU HAVE TO
SMILE FOR ME.

I NEED A PHOTO OF YOU FOR THE AUDITION...

WHOSE AUDITION?

End of Scene 33

TENSHI JA NAI!!
天使じゃない!!
てん し
シーン
SCENE 34

TRMBL

TRMBL

"A LIMITED-TIME UNIT WITH IZUMI KIDO".

IT'S A BIG PROJECT BEING HELD IN COMMEMORATION OF THE LARGE COMPANY "EZ GROUP"'S 50-YEAR ANNIVERSARY.

A ha ha! Heh heh!

TWO-PERSON TEAMS SHARE A CHANGING ROOM, SO I CHOSE YOU, HIKARU-CHAN...

LIMITED-TIME UNIT YOU CAN BE A STAR!

AUDITION SPANNING COMMERCIALS, SOAP OPERAS AND OTHER DIVERSIONS, IT'S A PROJECT TO DISCOVER NEW TALENT. IT'LL TIE IN WITH THE POPULAR VARIETY TV SHOW "HABAKURO9".

...OR THREE ...NK YOU.

DIRECTIONS

"YOU CAN BE A STAR!" AUDITION?

UH...

Now! To Uji!
WOOOO
I'm freezing!
Dragged along Number 2
Number 1

"That's right... Let's go to Uji!" A Little Trip Diary

In December 2005, it was just before a deadline that Shigematsu suddenly wanted to go to a famous teashop in Uji. So she pretended to finish her work and took her assistants with her to Uji. Even though by the Kyoto-Osaka train it's a distance that can be covered in half an hour... they didn't have enough time to fully explore Uji! See "Afterword" for the rest of the story.

I CAN'T GO DO THIS!!
AN AUDITION...!?
ME!?
ARE THEY EXPECTING A MIRACLE!?
WOULD YOU BE QUIET, TAKABAYASHI-SAN!?
GASP
S-SORRY!
AND...
...THIS WAS SUCH A SHOCK I NEVER APOLOGIZED TO IZUMI-SAN ABOUT SENSEI...
BUT IF I DON'T DO THE AUDITION, IT'LL PUT IZUMI-SAN IN A PINCH!!
SHARING A CHANGING ROOM COULD BE DANGEROUS!
AND THE HOTEL ROOM MIGHT ALSO BE THE SAME ONE!
BUT, I DON'T WANNA DO IT!
I HATE STANDING OUT!
I HATE AUDITIONS!

COME ON!!
GASP
S-SORRY!!
WAH WAH
Izumi-san...
CURTAIN
HMPH!
KNOCK KNOCK
YES?
HIKARU-SAN! WE HEARD YOU'VE GOT PERMISSION TO LEAVE...
Yo!
BUT WEREN'T YOU GOING BACK HOME FOR SUMMER VACATION?
WE WANTED TO INVITE YOU ON A PICNIC TO-MORROW.
CHISATO-SAN, MICHIRU-SAN...
I'M SORRY, I'VE GOT SOME-THING TO DO...

YOU'RE GOING TO A THREE-DAY AUDITION TRAINING CAMP TOMORROW!?
THAT'S AWESOME! SO THREE PEOPLE CHOSEN FROM THE TRAINING CAMP GO ON TO FINAL SELECTION ON TV!?
IT WORRIES ME THAT THE SCREENING CRITERIA IS A SECRET.
IRK
IRK
IRK
UGH, THEY'RE LOUD.
THE SPONSOR'S EZ GROUP... IT'S A REALLY BIG PROJECT.
AMAZING!! I'LL BE CHEERING YOU ON, TAKABAYASHI-SAN!
ME TOO, OF COURSE!
NO... WELL, BUT... THERE'S NO WAY I'LL WIN.

I'VE NEVER DANCED OR ARRANGED FLOWERS LIKE IN THE TRAINING CAMP'S SCHEDULE.
YANK
PATHETIC! ARE YOU NOT A FLOWER OF OUR SEIKA ACADEMY !?
I JUST DON'T HAVE THE KIND OF SPECIAL STUFF YOU NEED TO WIN AN AUDITION.
I- IZUKI-SAN.
I HEARD YOUR LITTLE STORY.
TAKABAYASHI-SAN, IF YOU AUDITION IN THIS STATE YOU'LL BE A SHAME TO SEIKA!
LOOK, UH...
BECAUSE OF WHAT HAPPENED WITH SEMPAI AND SENSEI, I OWE YOU ONE, SO...
THERE'S NO TWO WAYS ABOUT IT.

WE'RE GOING TO TRAINING CAMP, TOO...
...AND POLISH YOU UP SO THAT YOU CAN WIN!
HUH?
U...
...S?
Hikaru Takabayashi
Jan 1st
Girls' School
Sophomore
170cm
Weight: 54 kg
Special Skill: Walks
SO, PRODUCER SAKURA, I'M LEAVING THIS GIRL IN YOUR HANDS.

AKIZUKI-SAN, I'M NOT GIVING ANYONE SPECIAL TREATMENT.
EVEN IF YOU ARE PRESIDENT OF A BIG NAME AGENCY.
OH, YOU. I KNOW THAT.
HONESTLY, I JUST WANT IZUMI'S PARTNER TO BE CHOSEN WITH THIS ONE HERE.
THERE'S NOTHING I CAN DO ABOUT THE AUDITION.
BRIBES AND THREATS DON'T WORK ON THIS GUY.
IZUMI KIDO HAS THE PERFECT IMAGE FOR US.
SHE'S FRESH AND CLASSY, AND HAS NO MAJOR SCANDALS.
EVERYONE KNOWS HER FROM HER VARIETY APPEAR-ANCES.
REALLY...
...I WONDER IF WE'LL SEE ANY OUTSTANDING TALENTS AT THE AUDITION.

AT THIS THREE-DAY TRAINING CAMP...
...I'D LIKE TO GET A FEEL FOR EVERY-BODY'S QUALITIES FOR THE FINAL SELECTION.
THERE ARE CAMERAS ALL OVER THE TRAINING CAMP, BUT DON'T LET THEM BOTHER YOU.
EEE!
IT'S SAKURA-SAN! I'VE BEEN A FAN SINCE HE SANG WITH L.E.D.!
SQUEAL
YAY
WHAT AM I DOING HERE?
IF HE'S PRODUCING, IT'S A SURE HIT!
CHATTER
PLEASE JUST BE YOUR-SELVES.
AND ON TOP OF THAT...
...WHY ARE THOSE THREE STANDING THERE!?

MOVING ON. I'D LIKE TO INTRODUCE MY THREE NEW ASSISTANTS FROM THE NOTABLE SEIKA GIRLS' ACADEMY.
ASSIS-TANTS?
CLAP CLAP CLAP
I HEAR THE PRESIDENT OF EZ GROUP, THE SPONSOR, WAS ASKED TO HAVE HIS GRANDCHILD USED.
THERE ARE FELLOW SEIKA STUDENTS AUDITIONING HERE.
SMILE
BUT NO ONE GETS SPECIAL TREATMENT! BEST REGARDS!
CLAP CLAP CLAP
GULP...
I SUSPECT THAT I'LL BE GETTING SPECIAL TREATMENT, BUT NOT THE WAY SHE MEANT...

CHATTER
CHATTER
CHATTER
SO THIS IS THE THREE-PERSON ROOM, EH?
PARDON ME.
OH, COME ON IN.
SO, YOU'RE SHARING THIS ROOM, TOO? MY NAME IS AI UEDA.
Wow! She's so cute!
OH, I'M HIKARU TAKABA-YASHI...
K-CLICK
IT'S JUST TEMPORARY, BUT I HOPE WE'LL BE FRIENDS.
S-SAME HERE.

SAME HERE!
WHOA. ANOTHER REALLY CUTE GIRL.
LOOKS LIKE I'M LAST.
I LOOK FORWARD TO OUR NEXT THREE DAYS TO-GETHER!
I'M UEDA.
I'M KINO-SHITA.
I KNEW IT, ALL THE GIRLS AUDITIONING ARE REALLY PRETTY... THEY'RE FLOWERS! FLOWERS!!
NO MATTER HOW I LOOK AT IT, I DON'T FIT IN, HERE.
DROOP
SHAKE SHAKE
BUT I HAVE TO TRY! FOR IZUMI-SAN'S SAKE, TOO...
EVEN IF IT'S CRAZY, I HAVE TO DO MY BEST!

FIRST WILL BE WALK- ING.
CLAP
CLAP
ONE! TWO! ONE! TWO!
BACKS STRAIGHT, CHINS UP!
UGH...WHEN I THINK ABOUT THE CAMERAS, I GET SO NERVOUS!
THADUMP
THADUMP
STAAARE
STANDING TALL AND GRACEFUL WILL IMPROVE YOUR DANCING.
YOU THERE! DON'T HUNCH!
BACK STRAIGHT, CHIN UP...
STOMP
KEEP YOUR RIGHT ARM AND LEG OUT OF SYNCH!
GRRR
I- I'M SORRY!

YOU TALL GIRLS, TAKE THE MALE LEAD.
TRY NOT TO LOOK AT YOUR FEET.
MUMBLE MUMBLE
1, 2, 3...
1, 2, 3...
1, 2, 3...
I'VE NEVER DANCED IN MY LIFE...
I can't do it without looking at my feet!
HFF HUU
WHISPER
HEY, DID YOU HEAR?
WHISPER
1, 2...
HUH!?
WHISPER
ONLY THREE GIRLS WILL BE PICKED FOR THE FINAL SELECTION BASED ON THEIR GRADES HERE AT TRAINING CAMP!
WHISPER
HUH? REALLY?
SO, DON'T HATE ME FOR WHAT I'M ABOUT TO DO.
HUH?
TRIP
ひょいっ
THUD
!!
!!

OWIE...
YOU AGAIN!? TAKABA-YASHI-SAN!!
HEH
HEH
S-SORRY...
DARN IT...!!
AND JUST AFTER SHE TOLD ME THESE GRADES ARE THE DECIDING FACTOR ...!!
HEH
HEH
YOU OKAY?
-YEAH.
YOU DID THAT ON PURPOSE!
AND I HAVE NO IDEA IF IZUKI-SAN'S CHEERING ME ON OR WHAT.

OKAY EVERYBODY, BACK TO YOUR LESSON!
GRRRRR
HEH...
HEH HEH
IRK
I HATE THIS... THIS FEELING...
EVERYONE HERE, THEY'RE ALL LIKE THIS...
I MISS IZUMI-SAN...
I'D SAY THERE ARE TWO I HAVE GREAT HOPES FOR, SO FAR...

NUMBER FOUR-TEEN, AI UEDA
SHE JUST SPARKLES ON CAMERA... WITH A LITTLE TRAINING, SHE'LL BE GREAT.
BUZZZZ
THEY ALL BELIEVE THEIR GRADES HERE ARE THE DECIDING FACTOR.
WHICH COMPLETELY NEGATES THE VERY ESSENCE OF A TRAINING CAMP.
NUMBER SEVEN'S GOOD, TOO.
IT LOOKS LIKE SHE'S MODELED BEFORE.
PFFT!
WHAT IS IT?
SORRY. WE HAVE ONE GIRL WHO KEEPS MESSING UP.
LOOK, SHE'S IN THE TEA ROOM.
THE GIRL MAKING THAT COMPLICATED FACE?
I BET HER LEGS FELL ASLEEP.

AH, GUESSED RIGHT.
...THE OTHER GIRLS ARE AWARE OF THE CAMERAS AND EVEN PLAY TO THEM A LITTLE...
...BUT THIS GIRL HIDES FROM THEM, SO KEEPING ONE ON HER, WELL...
YOU... CAN YOU KEEP A CAMERA ON THIS GIRL?
OH... WELL, SORRY BUT WE CAN'T MOVE THEM.
AND...
HUH...
NUMBER FIFTEEN... AH YES, THE GIRL PRESIDENT AKIZUKI TOLD ME ABOUT...
FLAP
Hikaru Takabayashi
January 1st
Girls' School
Sophomore
170cm
Weight: 54kg
SHE'S CERTAINLY NOT WHAT YOU'D EXPECT FROM SEIKA GIRLS' ACADEMY...
SHE'S THE LEFT-OVERS?
WELL, THIS IS INTERESTING...

BLEEEEEEEEH!
THE ONLY CAMERA-FREE ZONES HERE ARE THE REST-ROOMS AND SHOWERS...
CHATTER
THERE'S EVEN A CAMERA IN MY BED-ROOM...
CHATTER
CHATTER
WHICH IS WHY EVERYONE SAYS WHAT THEY HONESTLY THINK IN HERE...
CHATTER
THIS IS MY EIGHTH AUDITION. I ALWAYS GET PRETTY FAR.
SO YOU'VE HAD TO COMPETE THIS MANY TIMES? DOESN'T THAT JUST MEAN YOU'VE **FAILED** EIGHT TIMES?
WHAT DID YOU SAY!?
SINCE THEY HAVE TO HIDE THEIR TRUE NATURES IN FRONT OF THE CAMERAS...
...THE STRESS REALLY BUILDS UP...
OH, TAKABA-YASHI-SAN!

CHATTER
I CAN'T BELIEVE HOW CROWDED THIS BATHROOM IS.
CHATTER
UEDA-SAN... YEAH, YOU'RE RIGHT.
STARE
UH-OH. AM I ABOUT TO SEE ANOTHER TRUE NATURE?
WH-WHAT IS IT!?
YOU'RE SO LUCKY... BEING SO TALL.
I... USED TO BE A MODEL, YOU KNOW...
BUT I HAD TO GIVE IT UP. I'M TOO SHORT.
SO THIS AUDITION IS MY TICKET TO A NEW DREAM.
YEAH?
AND YOU, TAKABA-YASHI-SAN? ARE YOU AIMING TO BE AN ACT-RESS?
WHO, ME!? NO...

UEDA-SAN! TELE-PHONE!
OH, SORRY. LOOKS LIKE I'M BEING CALLED.
BEST LUCK TO US BOTH!
WHAT IS THIS? I FEEL SO SUFFO-CATED...
はっ
DASH
I WANT TO SEE IZUMI-SAN SO MUCH!
AND IF I CAN'T, I WANT TO BE ALONE.
IF I STAY HERE ANY LONGER, I'LL CHOKE!

SNAG
!
AAH, THAT DOES IT! THIS DAY HAS KICKED MY BUTT!!
HNRGH?
IT DOESN'T HURT?
YOU ARE WAY TOO STUPID.
!?
DON'T YOU KNOW RUNNING IN THE DARK IS DANGEROUS?
COUGH
Y... YOU...
SHE WAS... LAUGHING AT ME IN DANCE CLASS...

TURN
TH-THANKS!
...YOU REALLY DON'T KNOW?
D-DON'T KNOW WHAT!?
LOOK, IF YOU'RE DONE WITH ME, I'M LEAVING...
SHHFT
YOU STILL DON'T KNOW WHO I AM?

WHA...
HUUUH!?!?!
IZUMI-SA--
MMPH!
YOU IDIOT! NOT SO LOUD! I'LL BE FOUND OUT!
WH-WHAT ARE YOU DOING HERE, IZUMI-SAN?
THIS IS JUST PART OF THE SCHEME.
SINCE I'LL BE JOINING A TEAM, I SLIPPED IN FOR THE FIRST DAY TO TEST COMPATIBILI-TIES.

IT'S NOT LIKE YOU'VE NEVER SEEN ME IN DISGUISE.
I THOUGHT YOU OF ALL PEOPLE WOULD RECOGNIZE ME.
IRK
H-HOW CAN YOU SAY THAT?
I WAS HAVING A REALLY ROUGH TIME!
YOU LAUGHED WHEN I FELL AT DANCE CLASS, BUT...
...THAT WAS BECAUSE MY PARTNER TRIPPED ME, OKAY!?
VENT VENT
EVERYONE'S SO CUT-THROAT HERE! I HATE IT!
BEHIND THEIR PRETTY-FLOWER FACES, THEY'RE ALL UGLY INSIDE...
THAT'S JUST BECAUSE THEY'RE DESPERATE.
THEY SHOULDN'T TRIP PEOPLE, BUT THEY'RE JUST FRANTIC.
.......!

I FINALLY GOT TO SEE IZUMI-SAN AND CAN'T CUT THROUGH THIS TENSION...
OH... OH YEAH!
I HAVE TO APOLOGIZE TO YOU, IZUMI-SAN... ABOUT WHAT HAPPENED WITH SENSEI AND SEMPAI...
APOLO-GIZE?
JUST LIKE YOU SAID, IZUMI-SAN, IT WAS THEIR PROBLEM, AND NONE OF MY BUSINESS...
YASUKUNI-SAN TOLD ME.
WHAT'S IMPORTANT IS TO KEEP MY PRIORITIES STRAIGHT.
I'M SORRY FOR GIVING YOU SUCH A HARD TIME...
....

WHAT PRIORITIES?
HUH?
WHAT PRIORITY FORCED YOU TO COME HERE?
LOOK, IF I DIDN'T TRY OUT FOR THE AUDITION, YOU, IZUMI-SAN, WOULD--
BUT YOU HATE IT, DON'T YOU?
MAKING ME PUT UP WITH THIS CRAP BECAUSE MY OWN GIRL-FRIEND DOES EVERYTHING "FOR MY SAKE"...
THAT DOESN'T MAKE ME HAPPY, DON'T YOU SEE!?

IZUMI-SA...
Tch!
WHAT DO YOU WANT ME TO DO?

CLENCH
SAYING THAT...
...WHAT DOES HE WANT ME TO DO...!?
IZUMI-SAN, YOU IDIOT!!
USING THESE IN-SEASON FLOWERS, TRY TO LET THEM BREATHE FREELY, PLEASE.
OH, IF YOU MAKE THIS A LITTLE SHORTER, IT'LL BE GOOD FOR IT.
CHATTER

GRUMBLE
GRUMBLE
DARN THAT IZUMI-SAN, DARN THAT IZUMI-SAN...
OW!
HIKARU-SAN, ARE YOU OKAY?
YEAH, I'M FINE.
WE HAVE TO GET THIS TREATED...
I said I'm fine.
DO THOSE TWO KNOW EACH OTHER?
THEY'RE FROM THE SAME SCHOOL.
NO WAY! HOW SNEAKY!
THERE. MUCH BETTER.
TH-THANKS...
SHE DIDN'T HAVE TO MAKE SUCH A BIG FUSS...
I'M SORRY... SINCE WE'RE FROM THE SAME SCHOOL...
...I WAS TOLD TO STAY AWAY FROM YOU TO AVOID ANY SUSPICION OF PARTIALITY, BUT...

OH! I'M SORRY, IT'S MY FAULT FOR GETTING HURT...
NO, THAT'S NOT IT.
TO BE HONEST, YOU LOOK SO UNHAPPY, I WAS WORRIED...
HUH?
THIS REALLY IS PARTIALITY, ISN'T IT?
I'M NOT CUT OUT TO BE A TEACHER.
CHISATO-SAN...
I'M SORRY FOR WORRYING YOU...
I GUESS I HAVE BEEN DEPRESSED A LITTLE...
CAN I ASK WHY?
WELL, EVERYONE'S PUTTING IN ONE HUNDRED PERCENT EFFORT, RIGHT?
THINKING THIS AUDITION WILL MAKE THEIR DREAMS COME TRUE...

SO TO HAVE ME, WHO HAS NO REAL DREAM, MIXED UP IN THIS...
...I JUST GOT SWEPT UP, AND THAT'S THE ONLY REASON I'M HERE...
BUT BY CHOOSING YOUR OWN PATH, YOU'LL MAKE IT ON YOUR OWN STRENGTH.
HUH?
YOU TOLD ME THAT, REMEMBER HIKARU-SAN?
WHEN I WAS WORRYING ABOUT MY FIANCÉ EARLIER THIS YEAR.
THERE'S NO NEED TO RUSH.
IF YOU'RE RIDING THE RAIL AND SEE ANOTHER PATH, IT'S OKAY TO TAKE THAT ONE, TOO.
BECAUSE WHAT COMES AFTER BEING SWEPT AWAY, COULD BE EVEN MORE WONDERFUL.

SORRY FOR TAKING THOSE WORDS FROM SOMEONE ELSE, THOUGH.
CHISATO-SAN...
THANKS... I FEEL A LITTLE BETTER...
GOOD WORK ON THE PAST THREE DAYS OF TRAINING CAMP, EVERYONE.
CLAP
CLAP
CLAP

I WILL NOW ANNOUNCE THOSE MOVING ON TO THE FINAL SELECTION.
IF YOUR NAME IS CALLED, PLEASE COME FORWARD.
SILENCE
GULP
NUMBER FOURTEEN, AI UEDA.
WHOA!
SQUEEEEAL
CONGR-ATU-LATIONS!
NUMBER SEVEN, KEI SAITO.
CHATTER
COMING.
AND THE THIRD PERSON IS NUMBER FOUR, TOMOKO MISHIMA.
Oh, wow!
CHATTER
EEEE! NO WAY!
CHATTER
CHATTER
OH WELL... IT WAS ALL FOR NOTHING...

BUT THOSE THREE TRIED THEIR BEST... AND THEY WERE GOOD AT DANCING.
THERE'S NOTHING I CAN DO...
ACHE
EVERY-ONE'S CRYING...

FOR THEIR DREAMS...
WHETHER HAPPY OR SAD, THEY'RE...
...CRYING...
SQUE
I'M JEALOUS...

AND ALSO NUMBER FIFTEEN, HIKARU TAKABAYASHI.
I HAND-SELECTED THE FOURTH PERSON FOR SPECIAL RECOGNITION, MYSELF.

CHATTER
THAT IS ALL.
CHATTER
NOMINATED PERSONS, PLEASE LISTEN TO A.D. FOR MORE ON THE FINAL SELECTION.
CHATTER
A FOURTH PERSON? WHAT IS THAT ABOUT?
AKIZUKI, DON'T TELL ME YOU--
NO WAY!
I DIDN'T DO ANYTHING THIS TIME. I'M SHOCKED, TOO!
THOUGH NOT AS SHOCKED AS THAT GIRL.
I... I WAS CHOSEN...?
End of Scene 34

TENSHI JA NAI!!

天使(てん し)じゃない!!

SCENE(シーン) 35

WHAT, ALL OF IT WAS THANKS TO MY SUPPORT?
IT LOOKS THAT WAY, I SUPPOSE, YES.
Hmph.
TO GET TAKABA-YASHI-SAN INTO THE FINAL SELEC-TION...
...I WAS A LITTLE HARSH.
I DIDN'T CARE WHO HATED ME FOR IT.
Ooooh!

I TOLD TAKABA-YASHI-SAN.
"NO SPECIAL TREATMENT. MAKE YOUR WAY TO THE TOP YOURSELF!"
THE AUDITION'S FINAL SELECTION WILL BE IN A FEW DAYS...
SHUT
SLINK
IZUKI-SAN'S TURNED OUR ROOM INTO A STAGE FOR HER SPEECHES...
AND WITH ALL THE GIRLS COMING BACK FROM SUMMER VACATION, EVERYBODY'S IN AN UPROAR.
CHATTER
WELL, EVERYBODY BUT ME, THAT IS.
CHATTER

よろっ
WOBBLE
THAT'S RIGHT...I WAS ASKED BY YASUKUNI-SAN TO SEND IZUMI-SAN A CHANGE OF CLOTHES.
RUMMAGE
IZUMI-SAN AND I LEFT TRAINING CAMP ON BAD TERMS.
FLAP
A PICTURE POST-CARD?
THIS...

WHAT'S IZUMI-SAN DOING WITH THIS PICTURE?
DON'T STAND OUT, YOU UGLY!
FOR HAVING THIS POSTER SHOT TAKEN, I...
Die, ugly!
I...!!

THE TRAINING CAMP WAS JUST AS I THOUGHT, A GATHERING OF CHOSEN ONES.

TAKABAYASHI-SAN'S CHANCE OF BEING CHOSEN...

...WAS TEN THOUSAND TO ONE!

BUT I KEPT PUSHING AND PRAISING HER AND NEVER GAVE UP!

オォォー!!

WHOAAAAA!!

It's increased

TAKABA-YASHI-SAN, GOOD LUCK WITH THE AUDITION!
THE REPORT ON THE TRAINING CAMP WAS INTER-ESTING.
OH, THANKS.
WE'LL BE CHEERING YOU ON!
THANKS ...

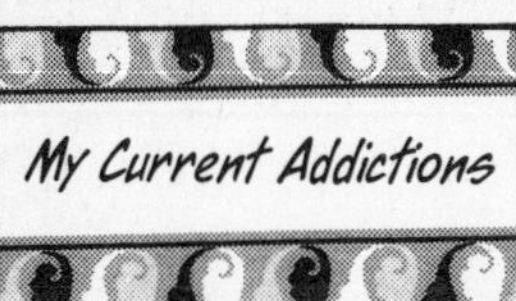

My Current Addictions

I bought the Hot Sandwich Maker I've had my eye on for a while now. Presently, it's getting rave reviews at my work-place. I can put ham and cheese in it... or tuna and ham... Actually, I've been meaning to try more creative combos in it lately...

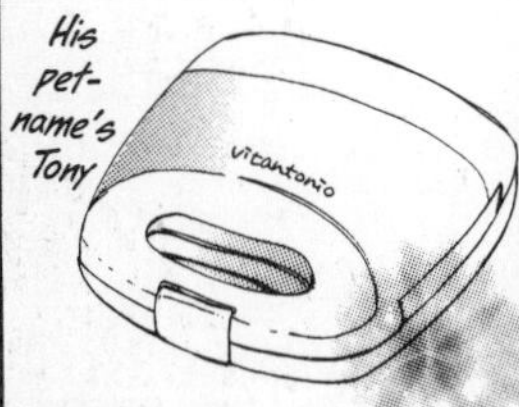

His pet-name's Tony

By the way, next time I'm going to make waffles with my assistants. And tai-yaki are also on our list of things to make. Tony's so great with his speedy cooking.*

**See translator's notes*

HAAAAAAH...
EXHAUSTED
HIKARU-SAN, YOU LOOK SO PALE!
WE DON'T HAVE TO DO THIS, NOW...
HUH? OH, NO, I'M FINE.

I HAD BAD DREAMS LAST NIGHT AND COULDN'T SLEEP.
YOU COULD'NT ?
YEAH...
OH, WELL THEN, HIKARU-SAN...
HM?
IF IT'S ALRIGHT, UM...
...YOU COULD PUT YOUR HEAD ON MY LAP AND SLEEP NOW...
FIDGET FIDGET

SQUIRM
UM...
SQUIRM
BRRRR BRRRR
Ah! A MESSAGE.
Message: I got off early today so I'm going home now.
RUSH
CHISATO-SAN, I'M SORRY. I GUESS I REALLY WILL DO THIS LATER.
IZUMI-SAN'S COMING HOME, SO I'VE GOTTA CLEAN HER ROOM.
RUSH
HUH? OH, I SEE...
I'M REALLY SORRY.
NO PROB.
I SEE... IZUMI-SAN, HUH?

OH, AND ONE MORE THING.
?
THANKS AS ALWAYS, CHISATO-SAN.
HIKARU-SAN LOOKS HER BEST WHEN SHE SMILES...
Hee hee!
Tee hee hee!

AIR OUT THE ROOM: CHECK!
BRING THE DRIED FUTON BACK IN: CHECK!
POLISH IZUMI-SAN'S FAVORITE TEA SET: CHECK!
--BUT ...
WOOOOO
WHY ISN'T HE HOME YET!?
HE SHOULD'VE BEEN HOME HOURS AGO.
GASP
MAYBE HE'S COMING IN THE BACK GATE?
DASH
OH, I WAS HOPING TO SURPRISE HIM!
SKREEECH

PHEW...
AND I HAVEN'T SEEN HIKARU IN SO LONG...
IT FEELS LIKE I'VE BEEN GONE FOREVER.
IZUMI-SAMA, I'LL TAKE THE LUGGAGE INSIDE. YOU GO AND GET SOME REST.
THANKS ...
WELL, WELL!

IF IT ISN'T IZUMI KIDO.
SEE? DIDN'T I TELL YOU? I *KNEW* IT WAS KIDO-SAN'S CAR.
PER-FECT TIMING!
WE'RE ABOUT TO PUT ON THE "AFTERNOON SEGEMENT OF THE PUBLIC PERFORMANCE ON THE TRAINING CAMP."
You're our honored guest!
DRAG
WE WOULD LOVE TO HEAR YOUR SIDE OF IT, IZUMI-SAMA.
NO, LOOK, I UH...
I'M SORRY, EVERYONE, BUT IZUMI-SAMA IS EXHAUSTED.
ENTER
YASU-KUNI.
QUIET, YOU **OLD MAN**!
STAB

OLD MAN
OLD MAN
OLD MAN
OLD MAN
24 YEARS OLD
NOW, LET'S GO, KIDO-SAN!
Y-YASUKUNI! SNAP OUT OF IT!!
GASP
IZUMI-SAMA!
CAW
CAW
OLD MAN...
MEANWHILE AT THE BACK GATE
ひゅううううう
WOOOOO
HE ISN'T COMING, IS HE...
THAT'S SO ODD...
I CAN'T BELIEVE HE'S NOT HOME, YET...

GASP
OH YEAH, MY PHONE!
OH.
No power.
OH, WELL
IF I WAIT HERE, HE HAS TO COME BACK SOMETIME.
AAAAH ...
FLOP
YAWN
BOY AM I TIRED.
I DIDN'T SLEEP MUCH YESTERDAY...
A LITTLE NAP WON'T HURT...
NN...
THE SUN...
IZUMI-SAN'S SMELL...

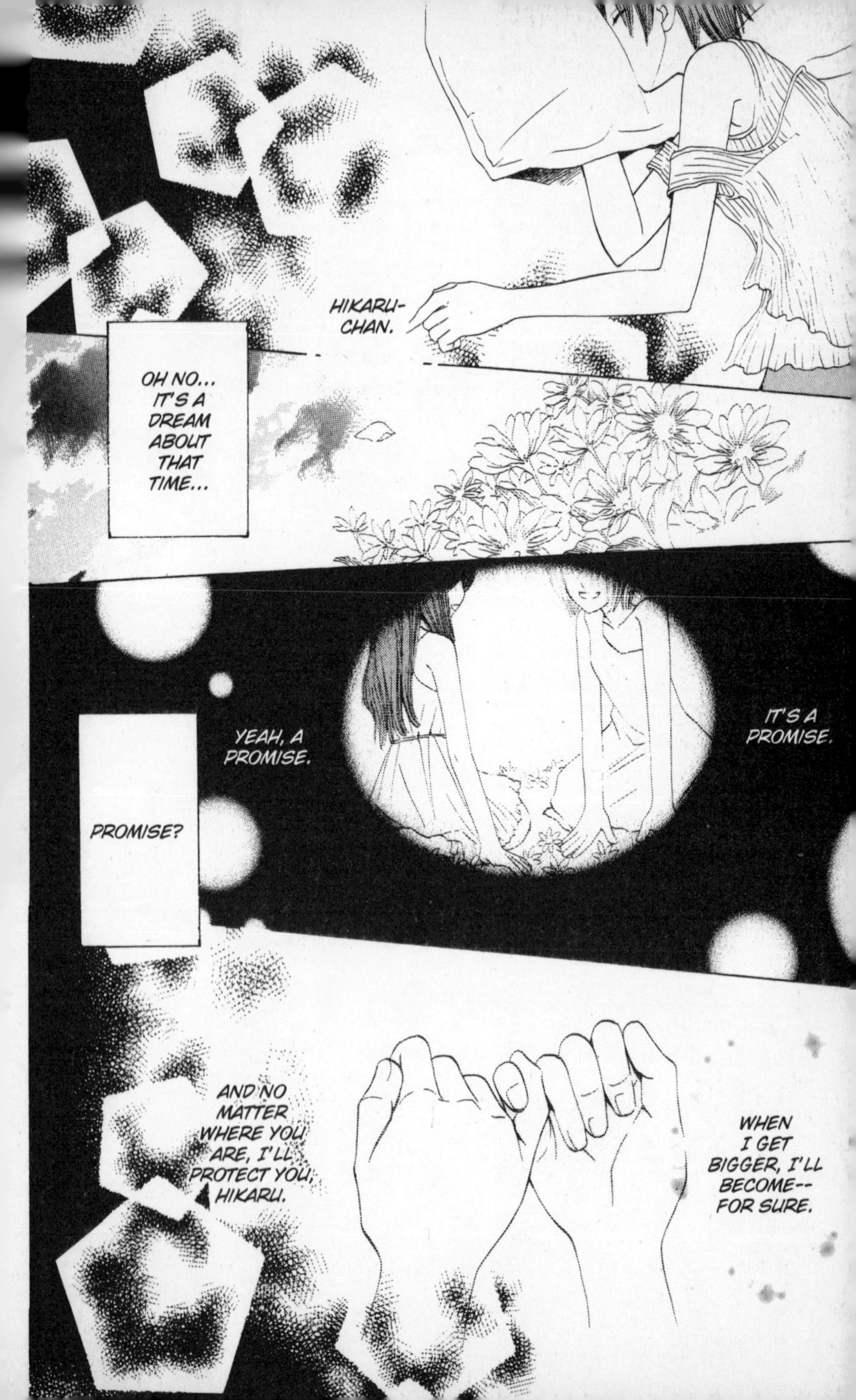
HIKARU-CHAN.
OH NO... IT'S A DREAM ABOUT THAT TIME...
IT'S A PROMISE.
YEAH, A PROMISE.
PROMISE?
WHEN I GET BIGGER, I'LL BECOME-- FOR SURE.
AND NO MATTER WHERE YOU ARE, I'LL PROTECT YOU, HIKARU.

PINKY SWEAR.

WHO WAS THAT?

DO I KNOW THAT KID?

K-CLIK

SO THIS IS WHERE HIKARU'S BEEN HIDING...

SHEESH... I CAN'T BELIEVE SHE'S SLEEPING WHILE I WAS HELD CAPTIVE BY IZUKI AND THOSE GIRLS...

RATTLE

SHUT

—

HIKARU?

SQUEAK

HEY, YOU AWAKE?

MMM... IZUMI-SAN?

HIKARU?
IT'S IZUMI-SAN...
THANK GOD...I DIDN'T LIKE... LEAVING YOU IN A FIGHT...
WE WEREN'T FIGHTING.
I WAS BEING SILLY...

LET'S STOP IT... WE'RE WASTING PRECIOUS TIME.
WE HAVE SO LITTLE TIME TOGETHER.
HEY, YOU AWAKE, HIKARU?
ZZZ
YEAH.
I'M AWAKE... IZUMI-SAN...

BUT I HAVE NO STRENGTH...
...IZUMI-SAN.
I WON'T DO ANY-THING TODAY.
A KISS IS MORE THAN ENOUGH.
NN...
I WANT YOU TO DO SO MUCH.
TO MAKE UP FOR ALL THE LONELY TIME WHEN I COULDN'T SEE YOU...

CHIRP
CHIRP
JOLT
I'M ALONE.
WAS THAT...A DREAM?
I THINK I DID SOMETHING REALLY EM-BARRASSING YESTERDAY!!
A dream!? A hallucination!?
BUT WASN'T IZUMI-SAN ALL OVER ME?

NO, IT'S OKAY. YEAH, I MEAN, WE'RE GOING OUT AND ALL.
BUT HOW SHOULD I BE WHEN I SEE IZUMI-SAN AGAIN...?
PUFF
PUFF
PUFF
I WONDER IF IZUMI-SAN ALREADY WENT TO WORK...
KNOCK KNOCK
K-CLICK
TAKA-BAYASHI-SAN... SO THIS IS WHERE YOU WERE SLEEPING!
SLEEPING IN SOMEONE ELSE'S ROOM IS AGAINST DORM POLICIES, BUT I'LL LET IT PASS THIS TIME.
MORE IMPORT-ANTLY, HERE'S AN AIR MAIL LETTER FOR YOU.
AIR MAIL?
YOU HAD YOUR MOM SIGN HER PERMISSION FOR YOU TO BE IN THE AUDITION, DIDN'T YOU?
OH, SPEAKING OF WHICH...

HI, MOM?
YEAH, I GOT IT TODAY. THANKS.
I'M SO GLAD I MADE IT IN TIME!
YOUR PROUD MOMMY ASKED YOUR BROTHER TO VIDEOTAPE IT FOR US, TOO.
UGH!
Y-YOU DID?
YES... YOUR MOMMY'S SO HAPPY FOR YOU!
HUH?
IT'S ALL YOU TALKED ABOUT WHEN YOU WERE LITTLE, HIKARU.
HOW YOU LOVED BEING A MODEL AND COULDN'T WAIT TO BECOME AN IDOL.
HUH?
YOU'D LOOK AT THE POSTER OF YOURSELF AND TALK ABOUT HOW GLAD YOU'D BE TO HAVE SO MANY PEOPLE LIKE YOU.

IF A LOTTA PEOPLE LIKE ME...
...I'D BE SO HAPPY!
CUZ EVEN IF I DIDN'T HAVE YOU, MOM, I'D NEVER BE LONELY.
I SAID THAT?
Heh heh.
AND YOU'D ALSO TALK ABOUT IT MAKING YOU RICH.
I DON'T REMEMBER THAT AT ALL.
AFTER MODELING FOR THAT POSTER, I GOT BULLIED AT SCHOOL, SO...
...I TRIED TO FORGET ALL ABOUT THAT TIME...
"IF A LOTTA PEOPLE LIKE ME" ...HUH?

LITTLE KIDS ARE SO SIMPLE...
THE DAY OF THE AUDITION
WELL THEN, GOOD LUCK, HIKARU-SAN.
YES!
PLEASE CHEER FOR ME FROM THE AUDIENCE, YASUKUNI-SAN.
TURN
NO...THE AUDIENCE IS JUST FOR YOUNG PEOPLE.
I'll cheer you on from the shadows.
?

I wonder what's wrong with Yasukuni-san.

K-CLICK

GOOD MORNI...

NGGGG ...!?

SILENCE

TENSE

TENSE

JEEZ, IT'S TENSE IN HERE!!

OH, UEDA-SAN?
LONG TIME NO SEE!
I'M SO GLAD YOU'RE HERE, I WAS SO LONELY!
YEAH, ME TOO.
She's as cute as ever!
Hmph.
WE HAVE NO TIME FOR THIS MUSHY CRAP.
PRICK
PRICK
THEY'RE JUST DEL-USIONALY OPTIMISTIC.
Ha ha...
I WONDER... IF I'LL MAKE IT THROUGH THIS AUDITION...
THESE FOUR ARE THE REMAINING GIRLS FOR THE FINAL SELECTION.
WE'LL DO OUR BEST!

AND YOU ALREADY KNOW THESE PEOPLE.
IT'S HABAKURO'S HABASHI-SAN AND KUROBE-SAN. AND IZUMI KIDO-SAN.
YO!
HI, THERE!
Omigod!!
I'M A HUGE FAN!
YOU DON'T SAY...
YOU'RE EVEN BETTER LOOKING IN REAL-LIFE!
U-um, nice to meet you.
JEEZ, WHAT A MOOD CHANGE!!
HEY, LONG TIME NO SEE, *HIKARU*.
CHILL

D-DON'T WHISPER IN MY EAR!
BLUSH
STEP
You gave me goose-bumps!
IS THAT 'COZ YOU FELT SOME-THING?
AH! IF IT ISN'T HIKARU-CHAN!
Long time no see!
OKAY THEN, I'LL COME GET YOU BEFORE THE SHOW STARTS, SO GET YOUR-SELVES READY.
SHUT
EXHAUSTED
SLIP
THE SHOW HASN'T EVEN STARTED AND I'M ALREADY TIRED...
THAT DAMN HABASHI-SAN, ALWAYS MAKING FUN OF PEOPLE...
Haah...
GRUMBLE
GRUMBLE
THEY'VE GOTTA BE KIDDING.
SO WHAT IS THIS? THIS AUDITION WAS ALL ABOUT CONNECTIONS?
YOU'RE PRETTY TIGHT WITH THE SPONSOR'S GRAND-DAUGHTER.
THIS WAS NEVER ANY KIND OF REAL CONTEST, WAS IT?

AUDITION, MY BUTT! EVEN IF I PASSED, IT'D BE NO GOOD!
IRK
IRK
THEN WHY DON'T YOU QUIT?
IT DOESN'T MATTER WHO YOU KNOW.
BECAUSE IN THE END, WITHOUT REAL TALENT, NOBODY WILL CARE ABOUT YOU AT ALL.
IT'S PERFECTLY NATURAL FOR PEOPLE TO USE THEIR CONNECTIONS.
THEY'RE SERIOUS.

IT'D BE RUDE TO THINK THEY'RE REALLY LIKE THIS.
IT'S JUST LIKE IZUMI-SAN SAID.
EVERY-BODY'S DESPERATE.
SINCE I WAS ACTUALLY CHOSEN...
...I HAVE TO MAKE A GOOD IM-PRESSION!!
SHUUUUUU
AND HERE ARE OUR FOUR FINALISTS!
FIRST IS NUMBER FOUR, TOMOKO MISHIMA!
CLAP
CLAP
CLAP

NUMBER SEVEN, KEI SAITO!
NUMBER FOUR-TEEN, AI UEDA!
AND NUMBER FIFTEEN, HIKARU TAKABAYASHI!

CHATTER
CHATTER
WHOA.
FIRST, OUR CONTESTANTS WILL INTRODUCE THEMSELVES.
SWEAT
WHAT AM I DOING HERE?
FREEZE
SWEAT
BLUR
IT'S SO BRIGHT.
MY FACE IS BURNING.
SWEAT
WHAT?
SWEAT
HUFF
HUFF
WHAT IS THIS? I'M EVEN MORE NERVOUS...
THAPUMP THAPUMP THAPUMP THAPUMP
...THAN I'D IMAGINED!!

CAL DOW
CALM DOWN.
YOU CAN'T EMBARRAS YOURSELF NOW.
CALM DOWN!!
OKAY, NEXT IS NUMBER FIFTEEN. GO RIGHT AHEAD.
HUH? G-GO RIGHT AHEAD WHERE?
SHOCK
INTRO-DUCE YOUR-SELF.
OH... INTRODUCE... RIGHT, I'M...
SHE'S ABOUT TO FALL APART!
I'M...
PANIC
...WHO AM I!?
PANIC

DON'T PASS OUT!
SMACK
AAW, SHE DID NOT!
PFFT!
YOU GET TOO NERVOUS.
I AM SO LAME...
I'M HIKARU TAKABA-YASHI. I'M SIXTEEN YEARS OLD.
Y... YEAH.
YOU'RE MAKING YOURSELF TOO EASY A TARGET.
You crazy girl.
BEST REGARDS.
Heh...
BUT, WELL...
...DIDN'T SHE WAKE RIGHT UP!

HERE ARE THE FIRST-ROUND RESULTS.
DA DA DA DA DA!
A LOT-TERY?
THEY WILL EACH CHOOSE A SITUATION CARD FROM HERE...
...AND ACT OUT AN IMPROVISED DRAMA.
WITH IZUMI KIDO-CHAN!
SQUEAL
Izumi-chaaaaan!
CLAP
CLAP
CLAP
NUMBER FOUR IS THE "BEST FRIEND."
RIVAL
NUMBER SEVEN IS THE "RIVAL."
NUMBER FOUR-TEEN IS THE "LITTLE SISTER."

AND THE LAST CARD IS...
LOVER
NUMBER FIFTEEN IS THE "LOVER"!!
End of Scene 35

"That's right... Let's go to Uji!" PART 2

So we got off at Uji Station. The moment we stepped off the train, we were struck dumb by Uji Station's futuristic design. The three of us made the quiet Uji Station into quite a thriving place...

I don't actually remember what it looked like so I can't draw it.

The circles! There are so many circles!

Beautiful!

Amazing!

...as we made our way to our goal of that tea shop. Taking about 10 minutes to find it from our simple map and then being saved by a married couple who happened upon us, we made it to the tea shop. And ate with much excitement.

It was delicious!

The green-tea parfait that the assistants ate, and the autumn green tea parfait were delicious!

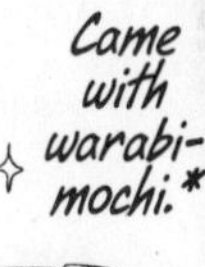

"I'm definitely coming here again!"

This is what we three vowed in our hearts as we ate our zenzai*. Next time we come, we're going to do sightseeing early in the morning and then eat chasoba*!! I bought tea as a souvenir on the trip home. It was a 2-1/2 hour short x3 trip (?).

*See translator's notes

Afterword and Special Thanks!

To all who read "Tenshi Ja Nai!!" volume 7, thank you very much! The messages appearing on my homepage's BBS have been not only from people in Japan but from Korea, Taiwan, and other places abroad and so this has served as a picker-upper for me. So that I can give a little of that picker-upper energy back to you, I'm gonna try hard from now on, too!

Also to my assistants who saved me, Hariguchi-san, Hatayama-san, and my manager who always suports me, Suguwara-san: thank you and the best of regards from now on too!

December 18, 2005 - Takako Shigematsu

I'm awaiting your letters

Go! Media Entertainment
5737 Kanan Rd. #591
Agoura Hills, CA 91301

Homepage URL is:
http://www5b.biglobe.ne.jpg/~taka_s/index.html

"TENSHI JA NAI!!" VOLUME 7 / END

Translator's Notes

Pg. 36 – *burusera*
A short-hand term combining the English words "bloomer" and "sailor" in Japanese pronunciation. This refers to the school uniforms worn in Japanese high schools and has also come to mean shops which sell young girls' clothing to dirty old men.

Pg. 157 – *taiyaki*
Literally "baked sea bream," this is a Japanese fish-shaped cake with red bean paste filling, though chocolate or custard can also be used.

Pg. 190 – *warabimochi*
A popular sweet in the Kansai area that is a translucent cool jelly with a soft and chewy texture.

Pg. 190 – *zenzai* and *chasoba*
Zenzai is a soft, sweet bean-jam dessert. Chasoba or "green tea noodles" are regular soba noodles that have been prepared with green tea powder.

As the story comes
to an end...

DID YOU TWO JUST ...KISS?

UH-OH.

...Izumi and Hikaru's *real* problems are just starting!

Find out what happens in the FINAL volume of

From the creator of "R.O.D.
TRAIN
+
TRAIN
Reiichi was on track to a normal life...
...until SHE derailed him.
go!comi
THE SOUL OF MANGA

AFTER SCHOOL NIGHTMARE

This dream draws blood.

"Enthralling!" – Library Journal

"An absolute must-buy! I haven't been this blown away by a first volume of a series in a long time."
– Anime on DVD

go! comi
THE SOUL OF MANGA

Author's Note

Thank you for picking up "Tenshi Ja Nai!!" volume 7! The reason why the illustration for the front cover looks so different is because I suddenly fell in love with copic markers (ha).

Visit Shigematsu-sensi online at
http://www5b.biglobe.ne.jp/~taka_s/